Clip Art for Back to School

Finally! The clip art book you have been waiting for! **Clip Art for Back to School** is a 48-page book jam-packed with several hundred pieces of art perfect to use to make your classroom a friendly, exciting place.

The vast array of art items contained in this book is perfect for all of your bulletin boards, homework papers, invitations, learning centers, newsletters and many more uses involved in the teaching profession. The possibilities are endless!

Also included are calendar headers for September and October. They look great when they are enlarged, colored with markers and laminated. Other special items include special awards to reward good behavior or work, borders to create notepaper and creative writing paper.

All the art contained in this book is printed on one side only so clipping directly from the book does not interfere with something on the back. Though it may be easier to photocopy what you need, so you will have it to use again.

So now you can relax when it comes time to be creative, because with our fantastic clip art book, all the hard work is done. Just clip or copy and enjoy!

1

SEPTEMBER

Sunday	Monday	Tuesday	Wednesday	Thursday	Friday	Saturday

Clip Art/Back to School   IF8628

September

My goal of the month is _____

SEPTEMBER

I reached my goal _____ # _____ times.

GREAT KID!

Chart's Purpose_____   Name_____

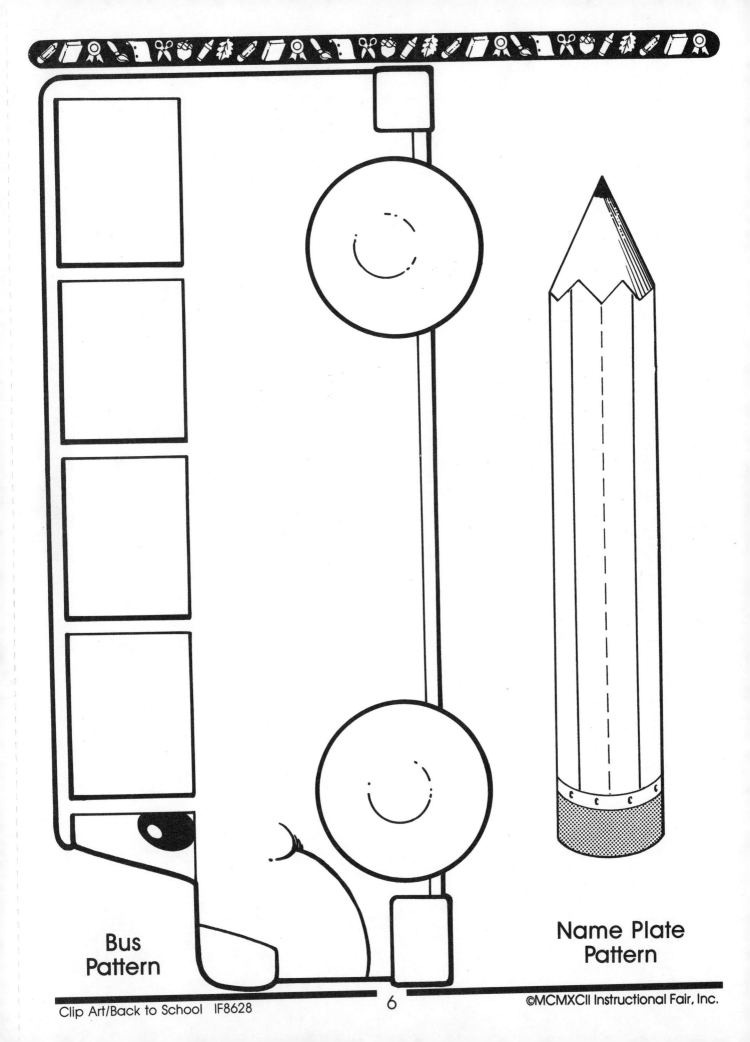

**Bus
Pattern**

**Name Plate
Pattern**

Clip Art/Back to School   IF8628

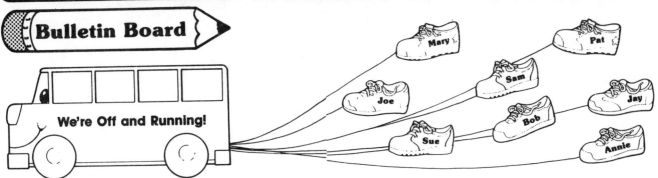

Bulletin Board

We're Off and Running!

1. Cover board with blue paper on top and brown or green paper on the bottom.

2. Using your opaque projector, enlarge the school bus on yellow posterboard. Outline it before cutting it out.

3. Duplicate the shoes on this page on colorful construction paper so there is a shoe for each student. Write the student's name on each shoe. Later, attach a picture of each student.

4. Arrange the shoes to look as if they are "chasing the school bus." They can even go off your bulletin board. Attach colorful shoelaces from the shoes to the back of the bus.

Running Shoe Patterns

Make one set of shoes to use as name tags on the first day of school.

Bulletin Board

Make colorful footprints to feature special students' work.

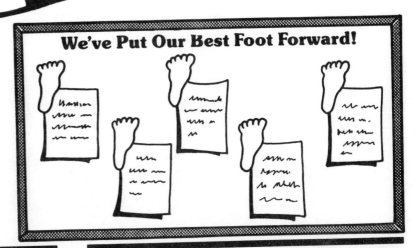

We've Put Our Best Foot Forward!

Terrific

GREAT

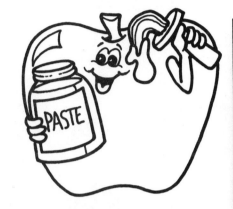

THE
COURTESY
AWARD

is given to

_____

For: _____

Clip Art/Back to School   IF8628

F E F

D E K

L J R

C D T

J P

P Q R

B C T

H O

N O P

A B G

H M

M N R

X W V U T S

4 3 2 1 Z Y

0 9 8 7 6 5

MY WEEK

Monday

Tuesday

Wednesday

Thursday

Friday

Back-to-School
Word Search

ALL ABOUT ⭐ME⭐

Name _____

This is me!
I am _____ years old.

This is where I live.

This is my family.

This is my favorite toy.

This is my favorite TV show.

year 2010

Here is my best friend.

Here is what I want to be some day.

15

Butterfly Bookmark
Pattern

MY READING DIARY

Book	Author	Comment

Shhhhhh!

CHECK OUT HERE

Music

GOOD EFFORT AWARD

Presented to _____

_____

Keep Up the Good Work!

Signed _____

Date _____

Clip Art/Back to School IF8628
©MCMXCII Instructional Fair, Inc.

Welcome

Clip Art/Back to School   IF8628   ©MCMXCII Instructional Fair, Inc.

Parent Connections

_____ needs to
work on _____

Please help your child
better understand by

_____
_____
_____

Thank you,

_____

Date

PLAYERS NEEDED

on our _____ team.
Our room is _____

_____

Players are needed to

_____

between _____ and _____
Let me know if you can help.

Thank you,

_____

MEMO TO:

FROM:

SUBJECT:

DATE: _____

_____ is working

on _____

_____

Please help your child
develop this habit.

Thank you,

_____

Date

Clip Art/Back to School   IF8628

Happy Birthday

Happy Birthday

Happy Birthday

HAPPY BIRTHDAY

HIP... HIPPO... RAY!

HAVE FUN!

HAPPY BIRTHDAY

to _____ !

It's my

BIRTHDAY!

You are invited to have
lunch with the ___ grade
in honor of

_____'s birthday.

_____ at _____
      date   time

_____
name   date

Happy Birthday
to a terrific student!

_____
teacher

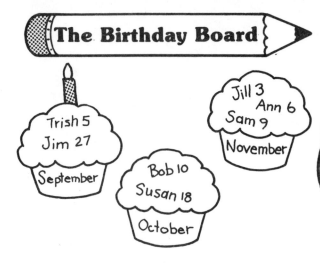

The Birthday Board

Trish 5
Jim 27
September

Bob 10
Susan 18
October

Jill 3
Ann 6
Sam 9
November

PATTERN

1. Using the pattern on the right, make 12 cupcakes.
2. Write the name of a month on each one.
3. On the icing, write the names and birth dates of each student born in that month.
4. Make a candle to put on the current month.

You could give birthday award badge to students.

HAPPY BIRTHDAY

Happy Birthday

Happy Birthday

Happy Birthday

HAPPY BIRTHDAY

QUIET!
BEAR
THINKING!
Shhhhhh!!

DAZZLING WORK!

_____
PRESENTED TO

_____
FOR

PRESENTED THIS _____ DAY OF _____ 19 _____

_____
SIGNATURE

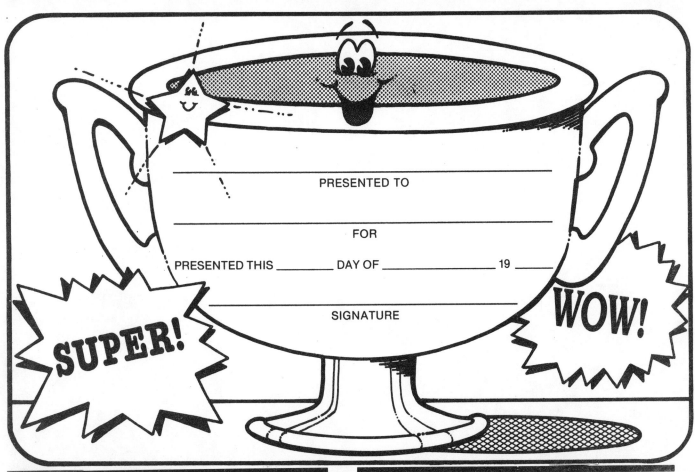

_____
PRESENTED TO

_____
FOR

PRESENTED THIS _____ DAY OF _____ 19 _____

_____
SIGNATURE

SUPER!

WOW!

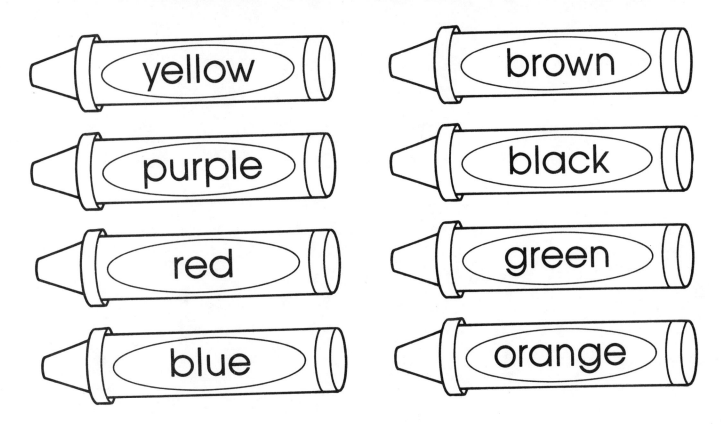

yellow

brown

purple

black

red

green

blue

orange

PRESENTED TO

FOR

PRESENTED THIS _____ DAY OF _____ 19 ___

SIGNATURE

WELL DONE!

RED

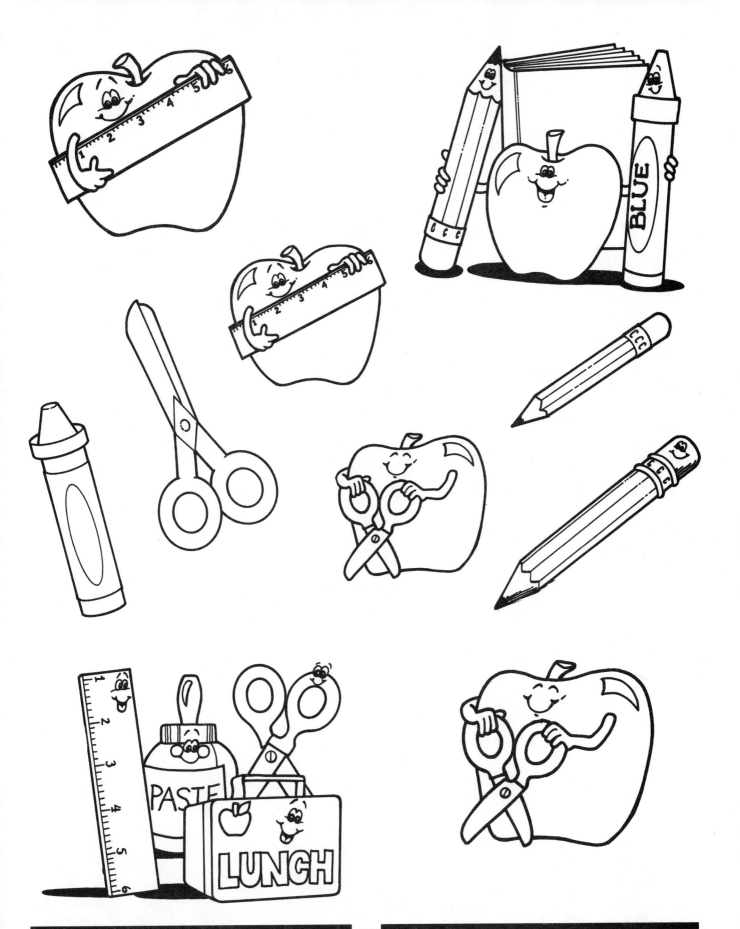

32

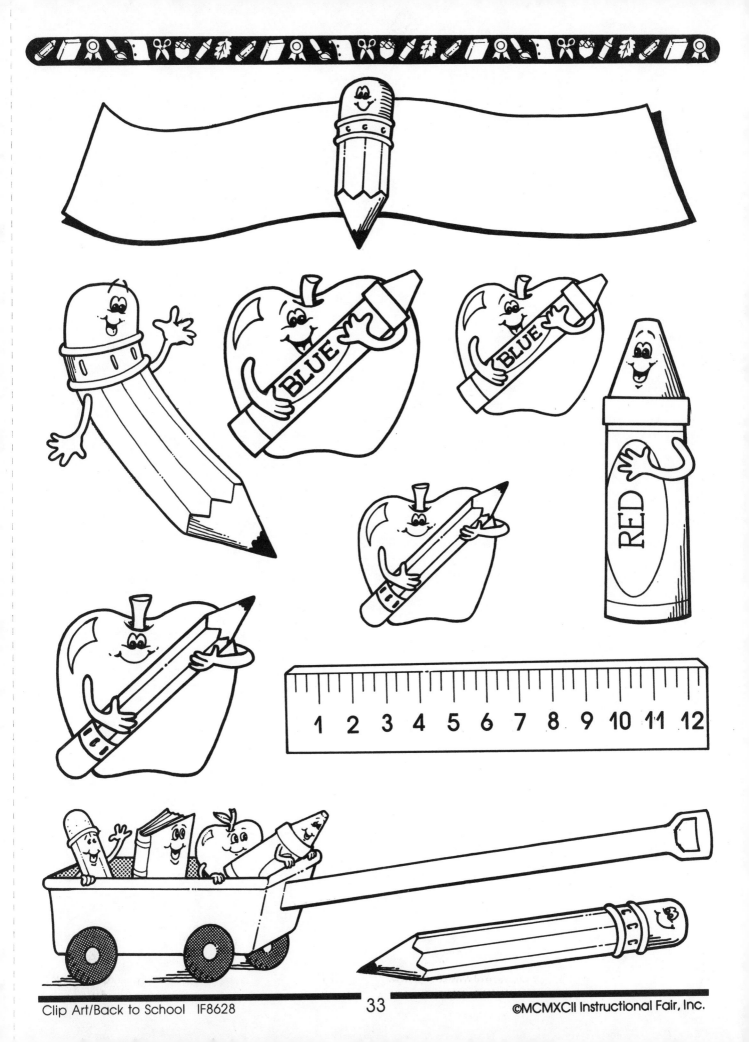

The Big Apple
Award given to

for

_____ .

Super Kid Award

TERRIFIC!

PRESENTED TO

FOR

PRESENTED THIS _____ DAY OF _____ 19 _____

SIGNATURE

SUPER STAR

S

AWARDED TO:

For:

Clip Art/Back to School   IF8628

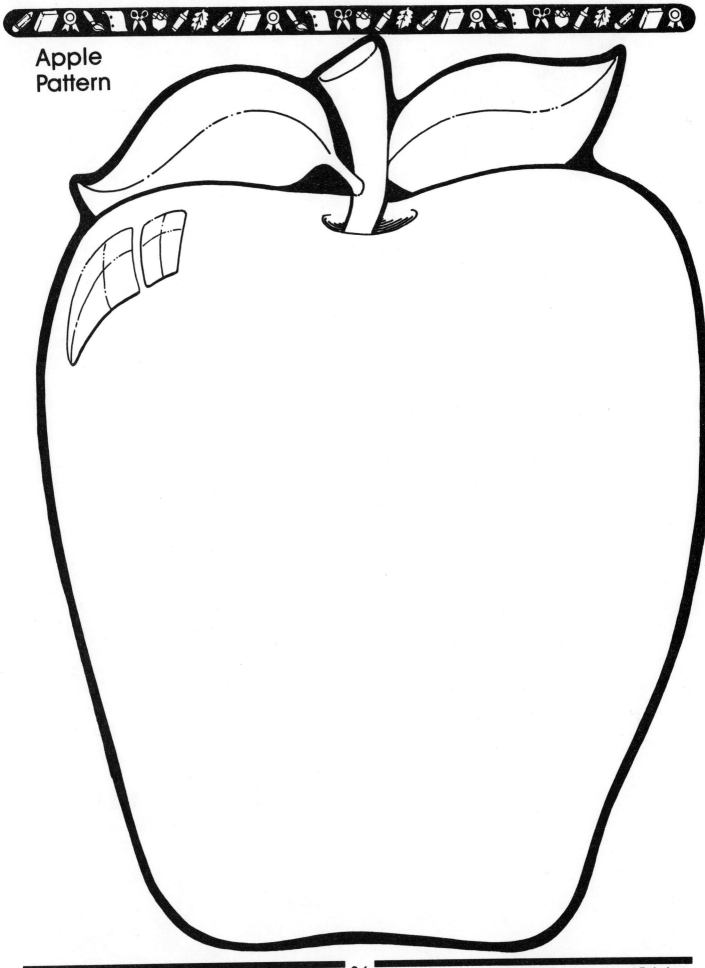

Apple
Pattern

36

My ABC's

A to Z

From

So PROUD of Me!

Name _____

Date _____

A to Z

A to Z

Johnny Appleseed Day
September 26th

Clip Art/Back to School   IF8628

Tree Mobile

Use a fall tree mobile for a variety of center activities.

Learning Leaves

Choose an activity from one of the falling leaves.

PATTERNS

1. Draw a large tree on colored paper and cut it out.
2. Punch five holes in tree and attach string or yarn.
3. Use the leaf pattern and cut out an assortment from red, orange, yellow and brown construction paper.
4. On five of the leaves, write fun activities for students to do in their spare time.
5. Place tree mobile on a board or on a wall.

Suggested Activities:

- Write your spelling words in ABC order.
- Write as many new words as you can from the letters in **SEPTEMBER** and **FALL.**
- September has 30 days. Write the even numbers from 1-30 in red. Write the odd numbers from 1-30 in orange.
- Draw a picture of 8 things you might see on a fall nature walk.
- Finish this story: I am a bright orange leaf on a huge, fall tree...

Good Work

Very Good

WONDERFUL

GREAT WORK

Use for creative writing.

Bulletin Board

A Squirrel's Tale

A creative writing board!

1. Make a large squirrel similar to the one on this page out of brown paper. Outline it with black marker.
2. Write the story starter on the squirrel: While I was busy storing nuts for the winter...
3. Place squirrel in center of board.
4. Cut colorful letters: **A Squirrel's Tale.** Place at top of board.
5. Duplicate the squirrel writing paper on brown construction paper.
6. Have students complete the tale on their squirrels. Display them around the large squirrel.

While I was busy storing nuts for the winter...

PATTERN

BRAVO

GREAT

42

OCTOBER

B**OO**tiful

JOB

NAME _____

DATE _____

No Bones About It!

You're Great!

Chart's Purpose _____ Name _____

Bulletin Board

"BOO"-tiful Work!

Use ghosts to feature special student work.

WONDERFUL

GHOST STORY

Name: _____

Reading Is Fun!

Cut out the
bookmark.
Color it.
Use it for
your
reading.